BEYOND
RUBIK'S
CUBE

HOW BIG IS

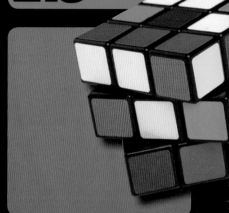

43

QUIN TILL ION?

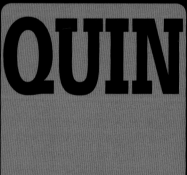

Lynn Huggins-Cooper

QED

QED Publishing

Created for QED Publishing, Inc. by Tall Tree Ltd
Editors: Emma Marriott and Jon Richards
Designers: Jonathan Vipond and Malcolm Parchment

QED Editorial Director: Victoria Garrard
QED Art Director: Laura Roberts-Jensen

Copyright © QED Publishing 2014

First published in the UK in 2014 by
QED Publishing, A Quarto Group company
The Old Brewery
6 Blundell Street
London, N7 9BH

www.qed-publishing.co.uk

Picture credits
(t=top, b=bottom, l=left, r=right, c=centre, fc=front cover,
bc=back cover)
01: Michael Wicks 02-03: t JULIAN BAUM/SCIENCE PHOTO LIBRARY, c
Kesu, tcr Michael Wicks, tr Hiper Com, cr Michael Wicks 04-05: tl
Michael Wicks, bl Ed Simkins, br Michael Wicks, 06-07: bl Getty
Images, c Kues, tr Yann, GNU Free Documentation License, br © Image
Asset Management Ltd./Alamy 08-09: l © Classic Image/Alamy, c
picturepartners, cr NASA, tr Alexander Kazantsev 10-11: l ©
Bettmann/CORBIS, b Vankad 12-13: l, c, r Kesu, tr fzd.it 14-15: tc
vrender, cl Kovalenko Alexander, bl jocic, br Luc Viatour/www.
Lucnix.be r Voronin76 16-17: c Reinhold Leitner, tc wong yu liang, tr
Sashkin 18-19: c videodoctor, bc cherezoff, cl Thomas La Mela, tc,tr
NASA, bl Ramon Espelt Photography, br Charlie Hutton 20-21: c
Neyro, bcl, bcr lynea, br DM7 22-23: r rui vale sousa 24-25: bl Jacek
Fulawka, tl, c, r Michael Wicks 26-27: bl public domain, c koya979, bcl
© SuperStock/Alamy 28-29: bl michaeljung, bc Feng Yu, r Getty

Images 30-31: bl © The Gallery Collection/Corbis, br © CORBIS 32-33:
br photofriday, tr beerkoff 34-35: tcl PavelSvoboda, tcr LiliGraphie
36-37: c public domain, bcl © Jinyoung Lee, tcr NASA, br © James
Horn, 38-39: tl Eldad Carin, cl PeJo, bcl © CORBIS, tcr Edward
Westmacott, tr public domain, br Hong Vo 40-41: cl Umberto
Shtanzman, c sellingpix 42-43: tcl MARK GARLICK/SCIENCE PHOTO
LIBRARY, bcl CNRI/SCIENCE PHOTO LIBRARY, tcr JULIAN BAUM/
SCIENCE PHOTO LIBRARY, cr Number001 44-45: tcl David M. Schrader,
cl SHEILA TERRY/SCIENCE PHOTO LIBRARY, cr JOSE ANTONIO PEÑAS/
SCIENCE PHOTO LIBRARY, tc Repina Valeriya, tr Iron Age/Getty
Images, tcr donatas1205 46-47: tc Vectorvault, bcl Getty Images, br
sippakorn, 48-49: c Sebastian Kaulitzki, cl STEVE GSCHMEISSNER/
SCIENCE PHOTO LIBRARY, tcr, r 3drenderings, bc DAVID SCHARF/
SCIENCE PHOTO LIBRARY 50-51: tc © Q-Images/Alamy, c ©
Moviestore collection Ltd/Alamy, bc © AF archive Alamy, b d13, br
vectorlib.com 52-53: tcl Ben2, GNU Free Documentation License, l UIG
via Getty Images, c Oleg Golovnev, b Eky Studio, tr David M. Schrader,

bcr sbchuck 54-55: bl Getty Images, tc Getty Images, bl © age
fotostock/Alamy 56-57: tc c Hiper Com, br Alexlukin/Shutterstock
58-59: tc Gyvafoto, bl Roger McLassus, Creative Commons Attribution-
Share Alike 3.0 Unported license, bcr tanatat, Delices, tr ©
Brownstock/Alamy 60-61: tl © Mary Evans Picture Library/Alamy, c
SSPL via Getty Images, tr SSPL via Getty Images, r PATRICK
LANDMANN/SCIENCE PHOTO LIBRARY 62-63: c Svetlana Foote, r
pzAxe, br GJ, public domain 64-65: tc sxpnz, bl sippakorn, bcr
defotoberg, cr AFP/Getty Images 66-67: cl Hans-Peter Postel, Creative
Commons Attribution 2.5 Generic license, bcr MikhailSh 68-69: bc
Sergio Bertino, tcr Christian Delbert, r © The Gallery Collection/
Corbis 70-71: tl, b Michael Wicks 72-73: cl Michael Wicks, bc ©
AlamyCelebrity/Alamy, bcl © Aleksandr Bryliaev, cr Imfoto, Roma
Koshel, r coutresy of Diamond Cutters International 74-75: tl Michael
Wicks, cl Getty Images, br photka 76-77: cl 00405-02, bcl courtesy of
Rubik's Brand Ltd, br GNU Free Documentation License 78-79: tl, br
Michael Wicks 80-81: br Michael Wicks

CONTENTS

IT'S ALL ABOUT **MATHS!**

This book will take you on a journey through the world of numbers – from **zero to infinity** – demonstrating how we use numbers and how maths shapes our world. To make sense of really big numbers, you need to relate them to your everyday life. Take the Rubik's Cube for example; it may be one of the world's most popular toys, but it's all about maths and numbers!

CUBES GALORE
The Rubik's Cube is made up of **26 smaller cubes** that can be moved around to solve the puzzle. Playing with a Rubik's Cube soon makes us think of really big numbers.

Take a Rubik's Cube apart and you can see how the corner and edge pieces fit into the central yoke.

Like any other cube, the Rubik's Cube has six faces, which are all square.

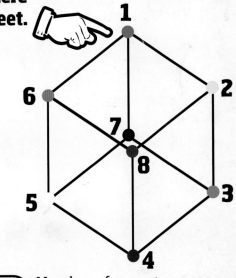

It has twelve edges where two square faces meet.

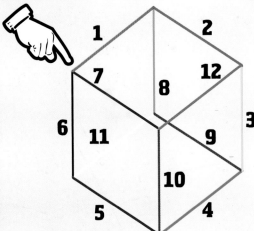

It has eight corners, or vertices, where three edges meet.

Number of ways to arrange the edges:
239,500,800

Number of ways to arrange the corner cubes:
40,320

The numbers start to get **really big** when you look at all the different ways the cubes can be arranged! And that's when you will discover just how big **43 quintillion** is.

Only another 43 quintillion moves to go!

ZERO

Zero is neither a positive nor a negative number - it means an absence of value. It is used as a place holder in many numbers, such as in the number **10**. Placing a zero after the numeral one changes its value to ten.

0

Negative Numbers
...-5 -4 -3 -2 -1

SPORTING ZEROS

There are other names for zero, especially in sport. In football (soccer) it is called 'nil', in tennis it is known as 'love' and in cricket a score of zero is called a 'duck'.

SLOW ON THE UPTAKE

It took some time for zero to catch on in Europe. Roman numerals were still favoured over Arabic numerals right up to 1500 CE. European mathematicians couldn't understand how a number could mean nothing!

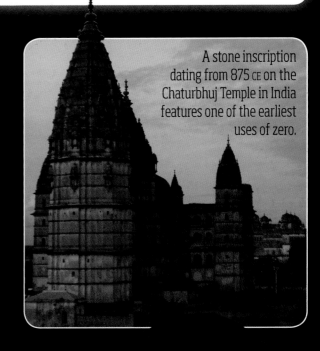

A stone inscription dating from 875 CE on the Chaturbhuj Temple in India features one of the earliest uses of zero.

Positive Numbers
1 2 3 4 5...

COMPLEX CALCULATIONS

Being able to use zero allowed Indian astronomers to make complex calculations that took their maths way beyond that of European scientists. They used their advanced maths to work out that the Earth spins on its axis and that it moves round the Sun. It would be another thousand years before the Polish astronomer Copernicus worked this out!

NEGATIVE NUMBERS

Any number above **zero** is a **positive** number, but any number below zero is a **negative**. Negative numbers have been around for a long time.

NEGATIVE HISTORY

The Chinese were using negative numbers in their mathematics as long ago as 200 BCE. Eight hundred years later, the Indian mathematician Brahmagupta created mathematical rules for using negative numbers. The Arab world continued to develop the idea of negative numbers, but the concept did not reach Europe until the 1400s.

In the 1600s, the English mathematician John Wallis created a number line that included negative numbers.

-5 -4 -3 -2 -1 0 1 2 3 4 5

NEGATIVE NUMBERS   POSITIVE NUMBERS

THINKING IN LINES

Any number above zero is a positive number. On the number line, they are counted up from left to right from zero. Negative numbers have a '-' in front of them and they are counted to the left from zero.

USING NEGATIVES
Today, negative numbers are
used for everyday activities,
such as measuring cold
temperatures and in banking.

Zero degrees Celsius is the
temperature at which water
freezes. Temperatures below
this have a negative value.

0°C
The freezing
point
of water.

-55°C
The average
temperature
on Mars.

-89.2°C
The lowest recorded
temperature
on Earth
(Vostok Station,
Antarctica).

People who
have a bank
account with a
negative value
are said to be
overdrawn.

-273°C
The lowest possible
temperature, known
as absolute zero.

100°C

50°C

0

-50°C

-100°C

-150°C

-200°C

-250°C

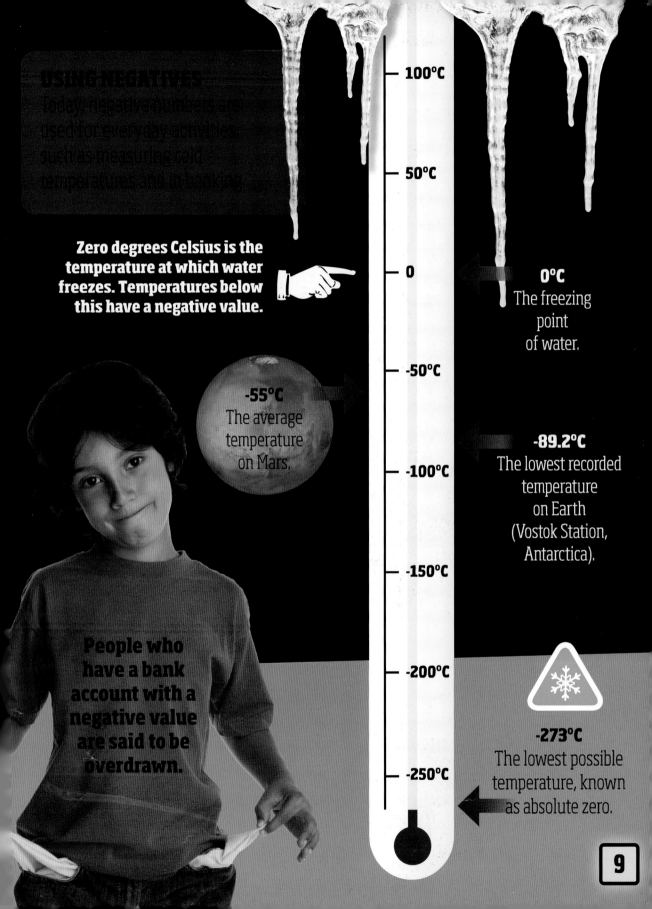

PLACE VALUE

Our entire number system is based on place value. The **position** of a numeral (or digit) within a number is crucial as it determines the **value of a number**. Place value helps us with our sums and without it addition and multiplication would be a real pain!

Fibonacci introduced the concept of place value to Europe, along with the use of numerals zero to nine.

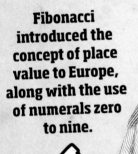

THE DECIMAL SYSTEM

Our number system is organized in tens and it is known as the 'decimal' system or 'base ten'. Counting uses the same numerals - from zero to nine - again and again. Once you reach nine, you start again from zero. The zero still means zero but when it is used next to another numeral, the value in the column to the left is changed.

Counting the ten fingers and thumbs on two hands led to the base ten decimal system.

1 2 3 4 5

Decimal comes from 'decimus', which is Latin for 'tenth', as this system of numbers is based on the number ten.

NUMBERS GREATER THAN ONE

Putting a zero after a whole number multiplies its value by ten.

So: 1^0 becomes **10** ...and 2^0 becomes **20** ...and so on.

Putting two zeros after a whole number multiplies its value by 100.

So: 1^{00} becomes **100** ...and 2^{00} becomes **200**

NUMBERS LESS THAN ONE

For numbers less than one, putting a zero immediately after the decimal point divides its value by ten.

So: $0.^01$ becomes **0.01** ...and $0.^02$ becomes **0.02** ...and so on.

For numbers less than one, putting two zeros immediately after the decimal point divides its value by 100.

So: $0.^{00}1$ becomes **0.001** ...and $0.^{00}2$ becomes **0.002**

WHAT'S THE **POINT?**

Decimals and fractions show numbers that are less than one. They are both ways of **dividing** a whole into smaller parts.

1 is **1.0**

½ is 1 divided by 2, or **0.5**

FRACTIONS AND RECURRING DECIMALS

Some numerators cannot be divided exactly by denominators.

⅓ is 1 divided by 3.

This fraction, ⅓, cannot be written as a decimal without recurring digits. It is:

0.33333333333333333333333333...

A fraction is made up of two numbers – one on top of the other. The 'numerator' is on top of the 'denominator'.

Numerator

Denominator

$\frac{1}{2}$

¼ is 1 divided by 4, or **0.25**

The number just keeps repeating. Mathematicians call this a recurring decimal. It can also be written as:

$0.\dot{3}$

Mathematicians understand that the dot above the number means it recurs indefinitely.

If two or more numbers are recurring in a decimal, then they all have dots over them.

So: $5.\ddot{1}\ddot{3}$ means   **5.13131313131313...**

13

COUNTING IN **HUNDREDS**

One hundred is not too hard to imagine. It is a big number, but we know it is made up of **ten lots of ten.**

One hundred

Zero tens

COUNTING MONEY

Many currencies around the world are counted in hundreds. The currency of much of Europe is divided into one hundred cents. Its name comes from the Latin word 'centum', meaning '100'.

COUNTING DAYS

The days in a year are counted in hundreds — there are 365 days in a year. That is:

3 hundreds

6 tens

5 units

CALENDAR

A person who reaches the age of one hundred is known as a centenarian.

0

Zero units

WHEN IS 100 NOT 100?
Senior officers in the Roman army were called centurions, and they commanded a group of soldiers called a 'centurium'. Even though these names may have come from the Latin 'centum', a centurion did not command 100 men. Instead a centurion only had 80 men – no-one knows why.

THINK IN **THOUSANDS**

A thousand is ten lots of one hundred: **10 x 100**. It is written as one followed by three zeros:

One thousand

Zero hundreds

If 1000 people lay down end-to-end, they would stretch for about 1.6 km, or four times round a running track.

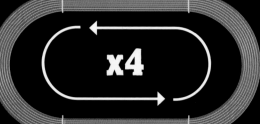

x4

Every day is filled with thousands of seconds!
One hour is made up of 3600 seconds and one day
has 86,400 seconds!

Zero tens

Zero units

AIRPORT
85 km

CITY
15 km

USING THOUSANDS

To describe 1000 units of length or weight, we use the term 'kilo'. Kilo means 'thousand'. So there are 1000 grams in a kilogram.

1000 g = 1 kg

A kilometre (km) is a unit of distance, and there are 1000 metres in a kilometre.

MAKING **MILLIONS**

A million is 1000 lots of 1000: **1000 x 1000**
It is written as one followed by six zeros:

1,000

One million

Zero thousands

THINKING BIG

Big numbers can be hard to understand. It helps if you think about everyday things, and what a million of them would be like. Think about a second, and how long a minute, an hour and a day are. Now think about this ...

- **A million seconds** is 11.6 days

- **A million minutes** is about two years

- **A million hours** is around 114 years

- **A million days** is around 2700 years

18

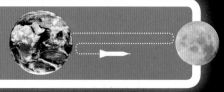

BIG CITIES

Populations of countries are counted in millions. There are about a million people in a large city. The world's biggest city is Tokyo in Japan, with about 8 million people living in its centre and 36 million in the surrounding metropolis.

Zero hundreds

Zero tens

Zero units

Imagine you have a million pennies. If you could stack them in a pile, it would be 1.6 kilometres high. It would be worth £10,000!

If a car travelling at 100 km/h could drive to the nearest star, *Proxima Centauri*, it would take more than **45 million years** to get there!

BRILLIANT BILLIONS

A **billion** is a huge number – a **thousand million**. It is written as the number **one** followed by **nine zeros**:

billions   millions

See how long a billion minutes, days and months would last for...

A billion minutes ago, the Roman Empire covered much of Europe and parts of Africa and Asia.

0 0 0 , 0 0 0

thousands   hundreds   units

A billion days ago, ape-like creatures, which scientists believe were our ancestors, walked about on two legs.

A billion months ago, dinosaurs roamed the Earth – it was the Cretaceous Period.

REALLY BIG NUMBERS

Trillion (twelve zeros)	**1,000,000,000,000**
Quadrillion (fifteen zeros)	**1,000,000,000,000,000**
Quintillion (eighteen zeros)	**1,000,000,000,000,000,**
Sextillion (twenty-one zeros)	**1,000,000,000,000,000,**
Septillion (twenty-four zeros)	**1,000,000,000,000,000,**
Octillion (twenty-seven zeros)	**1,000,000,000,000,000,**
Nonillion (thirty zeros)	**1,000,000,000,000,000,**
Decillion (thirty-three zeros)	**1,000,000,000,000,000,**

There are lots of big number names above a billion.

Light travels approximately 9.5 trillion kilometres in a year. This distance is called a light year.

Every time a number is multiplied by 1000 it gains three zeros and gets a new name! So a thousand billion is called a trillion, and a thousand trillion is called a quadrillion, and so on.

000

000,000

000,000,000

Estimates for the total number of stars in the Universe range from 100 sextillion to 300 sextillion!

000,000,000,000

An adult human is made up of roughly 7 octillion atoms.

000,000,000,000,000

000,000,000,000,000,000

Our galaxy is huge - with an area of around 700 decillion square kilometres!

A **BILLION BILLION**

A quintillion is a vast number – a billion billion. A quintillion is written as the number **one** followed by **eighteen zeros**. It looks like this:

1,000,000,000,
quintillion quadrillions trillions billions

If you laid a quintillion pennies out flat like a carpet, they would cover the Earth's surface twice!

EQUALS A **QUINTILLION!**

The Rubik's Cube can be arranged into

43 quintillion

(43,000,000,000,000,000,000)

different combinations.

0 0 0 , 0 0 0 , 0 0 0

millions   thousands   hundreds   tens   units

If you turned a Rubik's Cube once a second you would make:

 60 turns a minute

 3600 turns an hour

 86,400 turns a day

 31,536,000 turns a year...

If you started turning the cube when scientists believe the Universe started, more than **13 billion years** ago, you still would not be finished. To find all the combinations, at **a turn per second**, would take you **1400 trillion years!**

GALLOPING **GOOGOLS!**

The name googol was invented by Milton Sirotta, the nine-year-old nephew of mathematician Edward Kasner. Kasner asked his nephew to name a very big number - **one followed by a hundred zeros**. The name was published in his book *Mathematics and the Imagination* in 1940.

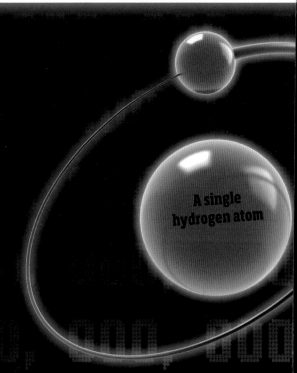

A single hydrogen atom

Edward Kasner

WHAT IS A GOOGOL?

A googol is not really used in mathematics, but it is sometimes used when talking about huge, unimaginable numbers of items. A googol is not the same as infinity - it is a finite number - but it is still huge.

There are over a googol possible chess games that can be played!

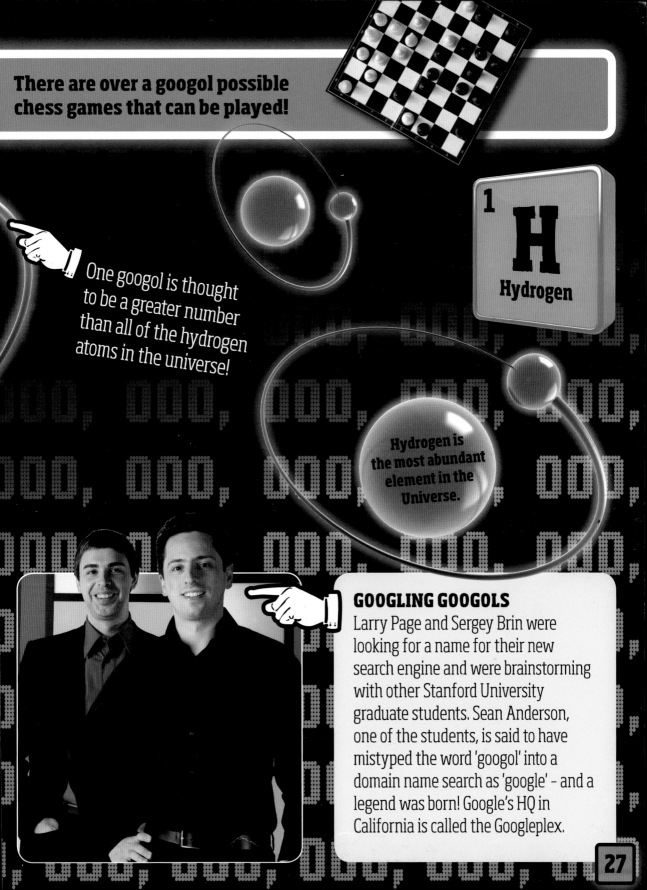

1
H
Hydrogen

One googol is thought to be a greater number than all of the hydrogen atoms in the universe!

Hydrogen is the most abundant element in the Universe.

GOOGLING GOOGOLS

Larry Page and Sergey Brin were looking for a name for their new search engine and were brainstorming with other Stanford University graduate students. Sean Anderson, one of the students, is said to have mistyped the word 'googol' into a domain name search as 'google' - and a legend was born! Google's HQ in California is called the Googleplex.

GREAT GOOGOLPLEX!

After naming the **googol**, Edward Kasner and his nephew Milton turned their attention to even bigger numbers. The next number they named was the 'googolplex'. Milton said this number was a one followed by writing zeros until your hand got tired! Kasner wasn't happy with this, so he changed it to a one followed by a googol zeros.

$$10^{10^{100}}$$

You can write out a googleplex using this mathematical shorthand.

You could never write out a googolplex in full!

A googolplex is a one followed by a googol zeros.

BIGGER THAN EVERYTHING

If you tried to write out a googolplex, with 50 zeros per line and 50 lines per page and if each book you wrote in had 400 pages, you would need 10^{94} books (that's a one followed by 94 zeros!). They would take up far more space than the whole Universe. Scientist Carl Sagan said ...

'... there literally **isn't enough room in the Universe** to write this number!'

COMPUTER POWER

Computer expert Frank Pilhofer pointed out that it isn't even worth getting a computer to print out a googolplex. As computers become more powerful, any computer that started to print out the number would eventually be overtaken by a more powerful one, which would also be overtaken by a more powerful one, and so on, and so on...

EVEN BIGGER NUMBERS!

But a googolplex isn't the biggest number to be named. That title belongs to the googolplexplex, which is a one followed by a googolplex of zeros!

THE IDEA OF INFINITY

Infinity is not really a number - it is an idea or mathematical concept. **You can't count to infinity**. Infinity means endless or something that has no limits.

Galileo lived from
1564 to 1642.

GALILEO'S PARADOX

In the 1600s , Italian scientist Galileo produced some puzzling ideas about infinity. He took two sets of numbers that go on for ever - **counting numbers** (1, 2, 3, etc...) and **square numbers** (1, 2, 4, 9, etc). Not all counting numbers are square numbers, so there are more counting numbers than square numbers - right? **Wrong!** Every square number is made by multiplying two counting numbers together, so there has to be the same number of square numbers as counting numbers! It's enough to make your brain ache!

The infinity symbol looks like a number eight tipped on its side. It was first used by English mathematician John Wallis in 1655.

Astronomers have shown that not even the Universe is infinite. In fact, scientists have now calculated that the Universe measures 93 billion light years across. But that's nowhere near as big as infinity, which goes on for ever, and ever, and ever, and ever...

This image was taken by the Hubble Space Telescope and it shows millions of galaxies that are billions of light years away.

BIGGER THAN INFINITY

In the 1870s, **Georg Cantor** developed a theory of **transfinite arithmetic** - the maths of numbers beyond infinity. He spent many years trying to prove this theory, without success.

STATISTICS

Statistics are used by mathematicians to **collect, summarise** and **interpret** large figures or data collected by researchers. This enormous collection of **facts and figures** can then be used to describe groups of numbers, to support ideas, and to help make vital decisions.

Statistics can be shown using different charts and diagrams, such as a pie chart (right) and a bar chart (far right).

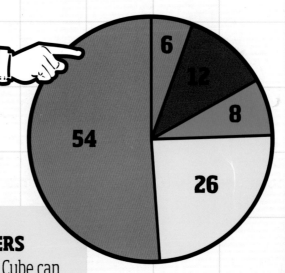

RUBIK'S CUBE NUMBERS

Statistics about the Rubik's Cube can be represented graphically in lots of different ways:

Number of sides = **6**
Number of corners = **8**
Number of edges = **12**
Number of pieces = **26**
Number of coloured squares = **54**

At the peak of its popularity in the 1980s, it is estimated that one-fifth of the world's population had played with the Rubik's Cube.

USING STATISTICS

In medicine, statistics may help hospitals to decide **how to use their resources.** For example, if statistics show that a lot of patients need surgery for heart problems rather than other problems, people can use the information to spend more money on heart procedures.

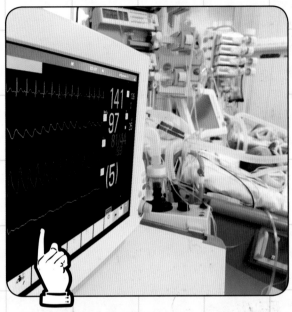

Medical equipment, such as this ECG machine, is expensive, so hospitals need to plan carefully how to use their resources.

Stock market displays show a range of figures, including prices and the number of shares that have been bought and sold.

COUNTING THE COST

Statistics are also used by bankers and traders to **track patterns** and **trends** in the **money markets**. This helps them to predict future movements and figure out where best to invest their money. Huge sums – in the form of stocks, shares and bonds – are traded in the **stock markets** of big cities such as London and New York.

COUNTING PEOPLE

The population of a country is the **number of people who live there**. Population numbers can be really big - **millions** or even **billions** of people.

Greenland has just **0.03 people** per square kilometre.

Most countries use a census to count their population. The information in a census tells us a great deal about the history of people who lived before us. **According to a 2011 census, the UK population is around 63, 182,000** - sixty-three million, one hundred and eighty-two thousand. That makes it the third largest population in the European Union, and the 22nd largest population in the world.

Top five largest countries by population size

China 1.351 billion

The population of the world in 2013 was 7.162 billion.

Monaco
has more than
18,000 people
per square kilometre.

The number of people living in a particular area is the **population density**, and this varies greatly from one place to another. Some countries are crammed full of people, while others have huge areas where almost no one lives at all.

India
1.237 billion

USA
313.9 million

Indonesia
246.9 million

Brazil
201 million

BIG NUMBERS **IN SPACE**

Big numbers are used to describe the vast distances of space, often in terms of **'light years'**. A light year is the distance that light can travel in a year – nearly 10 trillion km.

USING LIGHT YEARS

Astronomers use light years to measure the distance to stars and other space objects. Light from some of the most distant objects we can spot left those objects billions of years ago – before the Earth had formed!

Light travelling from the Sun takes **eight minutes** to reach us.

QUICK AS A FLASH!

Light travels very quickly – at nearly **300,000 km per second**. Travelling at the speed of light, you could circle the Earth about eight times in a single second!

Think about this the next time there's a thunderstorm. You will see the bright lightning flash before you hear the thunder because **light travels more quickly than sound**.

The Orion Nebula is a huge cloud of glowing gas that is more than 1300 light years from Earth - that's more than 13,000 trillion kilometres (13 quadrillion kilometres)!

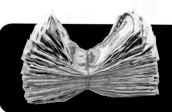

STACKS OF CASH

The money supply of a country is made up of **banknotes** and **coins**, known as **'currency'**. These notes and coins represent value but are **not worth anything** in themselves, as the materials they are made from are not expensive - banknotes are made from paper or plastic and coins are now made from non-precious metals.

A German 10 million mark note

During the 1920s, Germany suffered from massive inflation because the country was in a **lot of debt** after World War I. The government printed notes with bigger values, but these quickly became worthless.

This woman is lighting a fire with worthless banknotes.

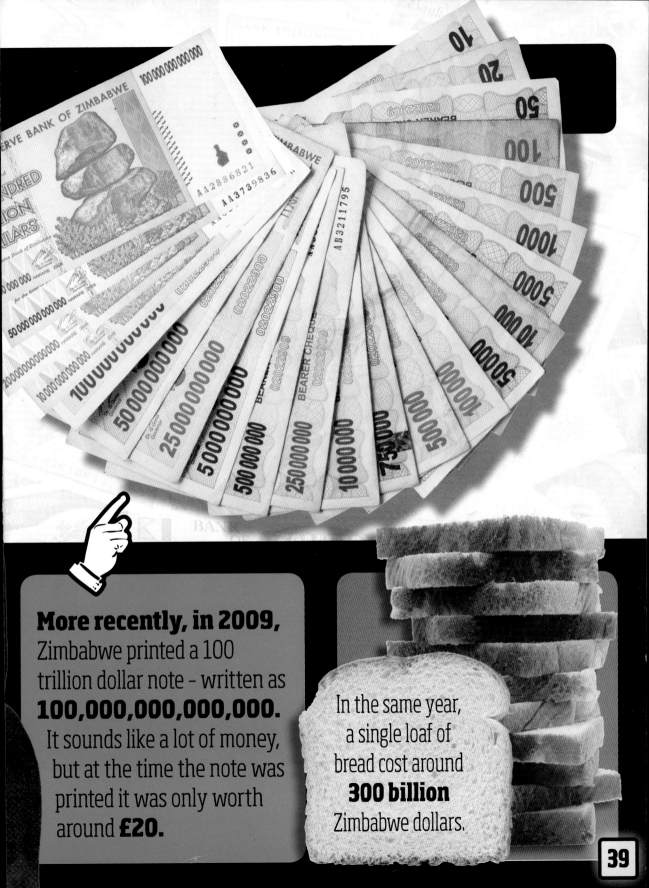

More recently, in 2009, Zimbabwe printed a 100 trillion dollar note - written as **100,000,000,000,000.** It sounds like a lot of money, but at the time the note was printed it was only worth around **£20.**

In the same year, a single loaf of bread cost around **300 billion** Zimbabwe dollars.

GLOBAL NUMBERS

The Earth is a large ball, or **sphere**. In fact, it's actually a squashed sphere and is wider around the **middle** than it is around the **poles**.

OCEANS

About 149 million km² of the Earth's surface is land, but that's just over 29 per cent. The rest is water, mostly in the form of oceans, and nearly half of this (46.5%) is made up of the Pacific Ocean alone.

46.5% Pacific Ocean

EQUATOR

This is the imaginary line that runs around the middle of the Earth. It divides the planet into the Northern and Southern hemispheres. The circumference of the Earth at the equator is around **40,075 kilometres**.

POLE TO POLE

The distance between the North Pole and the South Pole is a little more than 20,000 kilometres 'as the crow flies' - which means travelling in a straight line.

North Pole

20,000 kilometres

12,800 kilometres

South Pole

However, if you tunnelled straight through the centre of the Earth from pole to pole, the distance would be a mere 12,800 kilometres!

4.1% Arctic Ocean

22.9% Atlantic Ocean

START AND FINISH

SAILING ROUND THE WORLD

If you were sailing in the Vendée Globe round-the-world yacht race, your route would have to be a lot longer than the distance around the equator, because you would have to avoid the continents.

Equator

20.5% Indian Ocean

6% Southern Ocean

Sailing the Vendée Globe race would see you travelling about 30,000 nautical miles (around 55,000 kilometres).

FROM THE **BIG BANG**

Scientists believe that the **Universe** started **billions** of years ago with a big bang. Discover what happened after that, and when...

The Sun

3.8 billion years ago
the first living cells appear on Earth.

700 million years ago
primitive life appears, such as flatworms and algae.

85 million years ago
dinosaurs become extinct.

200 million years ago
the first mammals appear.

15 million years ago
the great apes or Hominidae appear.

600,000 years ago
humans' early ancestors
Homo heidelbergensis appear.

... TO THE FIRST PEOPLE

13.8 billion years ago
the Big Bang is believed
to have happened.

**300 million years
after the Big Bang**
stars and galaxies form.

About 4.5 billion years ago
the Earth forms from the debris
that swirls around the Sun.

5 billion years ago
the Sun is born.

570 million years ago
creatures with hard shells appear.

231.4 million years ago
dinosaurs first appear.

**200,000 years ago *Homo sapiens*,
the first 'modern' people, emerge.**

PREHISTORIC TIMES

Historians and archaeologists talk about prehistory - the **Stone Age,** the **Bronze Age** and the **Iron Age**. These periods are named after the artefacts left behind.

The Stone Age covered a long period and dates back to the first time the ancestors of modern humans used tools. There is evidence that Stone Age people lived in caves, as can be seen at the Bhimbetka rock shelters in India.

The first tools were made of stone. Fossilised animal bones bearing marks made by stone tools have been found in Ethiopia. At 3.4 million years old, they are the earliest evidence of stone tools.

A stone tool made around 6000 BCE

THE BRONZE AGE

3300 BCE

6000 BCE

THE STONE AGE

2500 BCE

Iron age tools 👉

The Bronze Age began in the Middle East, the Indus Valley and Southeast Asia in around 3300 BCE. Over the next thousand years, it spread into Ancient Egypt, Europe and Britain.

The Iron Age started around 3000 years ago. Iron and steel artefacts dating to this time can be seen in many museums.

 This bronze and gold disc showing the Sun, Moon and stars was made around 1600 BCE, during the Bronze Age.

700 BCE

1000 BCE

THE IRON AGE

400 BCE

COUNTING DAYS

We split the **year** into different periods – **months**, **weeks** and **days**. Throughout history, different civilisations have used different numbering systems to divide the year.

365 days = one year!

GREGORIAN CALENDAR
In the western world, the Gregorian calendar is used. It was named after the man who introduced it in **1582, Pope Gregory XIII**. It is a solar calendar, based on a **365-day year**, divided into **12 months**. It was designed by Luigi Lilio Ghiraldi, an astronomer and doctor.

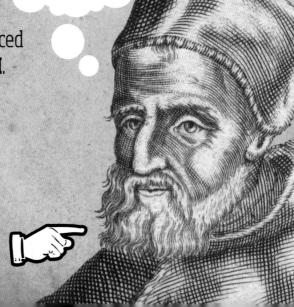

Pope Gregory XIII

MAYAN CALENDAR

Until the 16th century, most cultures in Central America used the Mayan calendar. Developed in 2000 BCE and still in use in some communities today, it uses a combination of cycles lasting **260 days** and **365 days**, to create a longer cycle lasting for **18,980 days**, or **52 years of 365 days**.

The symbols, or glyphs, on this wheel represent the days of the different Mayan calendar cycles.

The Chinese New Year is celebrated on a different day each year.

CHINESE CALENDAR

The Chinese calendar is based on exact astronomical observations of the Sun's movement and the Moon's phases. An ordinary Chinese year has **12 months**, while a leap year has 13 months.

YOUR **AMAZING BODY**

Have you any idea how **amazing** your body is? There are some **really big numbers** involved. For example, an adult's body contains about **34 trillion** tiny cells!

Nerve cells are the longest cells in your body. They carry signals between your central nervous system and your organs and limbs.

HEADFUL OF HAIR

Do you know how many hairs there are on your head? It depends on the colour of your hair:

Hairs grow out of tiny pits in your skin called follicles. The shape of the follicle determines if the hair is straight, wavy or curly.

If you have red hair, you have around 90,000 hairs.

If you have black hair, you have around 108,000 hairs.

If you have brown hair, you have around 110,000 hairs.

If you have blonde hair, you could have up to 140,000 hairs.

An adult human has around two square metres of skin.

COUNTING BONES

You contain lots of bones, too. **When you are born, you have 350 bones**, but some of these fuse together as you grow. **By the time you are an adult, you will have 206 bones**.

An adult skeleton has:

- **22 bones in the skull**
- **26 vertebrae in the spine**
- **24 ribs**
- **27 bones in each hand**

The longest bone is the **femur** (thigh bone) and the smallest is the **stirrup** in the ear.

Around 1000 species of bacteria can be found on the skin – but luckily most of them do not make us ill.

BILLIONS OF BACTERIA

The average human has around 1 trillion bacteria on their skin! These are mainly found in the hair follicles and on the epidermis layer.

BIG BUDGETS, BIG FILM$

HARRY POTTER AND THE HALF-BLOOD PRINCE

PIRATES OF THE CARIBBEAN: AT WORLD'S END

TANGLED

Big movies need big stars. This list shows the total earnings of the biggest film stars of all time.

⭐ 1. Harrison Ford............. **US$7.4 bn**
⭐ 2. Tom Hanks................. **US$6.2 bn**
⭐ 3. Eddie Murphy............ **US$5.9 bn**
⭐ 4. Tom Cruise................. **US$5 bn**
⭐ 5. Robin Williams.......... **US$4.8 bn**

Did you know that a huge amount of money is spent making the films we watch? The film studios take a risk. But compare the money spent (the budget) on these films with the money they earned at the box office!

US$250 million to make

US$934 million at the box office

Profit US$684 million

US$300 million to make

US$960 million at the box office

Profit US$660 million

US$260 million to make

US$586 million at the box office

Profit US$326 million

Even though these movies took lots of money, they are not the most profitable ever made. Disney's *Peter Pan* (1953) cost US$4 million to make, but made a profit of more than **US$140 million** - a return of nearly **3500 per cent**!

A HISTORY OF **NUMBERS**

The first evidence we have of people counting is **thousands of years old**. The Ishango Bone was found in Africa in 1960. Notches cut into this baboon's leg bone indicate something was being **counted** – although we do not know what.

The Ishango Bone is about 20,000 years old.

Sumerian clay tablet

EARLY MATHS

When people first began gathering together in cities, numbers and counting were needed to help them **organise things** such as livestock. In around 4000 BCE, people in the ancient empire of Sumeria wrote mathematical **sums on clay tablets**. Those who kept track of the tablets were the world's first accountants!

$$\text{↙} = 10 \quad \text{↓} = 1$$

$$\text{↓↓} + \text{↙} = \text{↙↓↓}$$

$$2 + 10 = 12$$

The Sumerians combined differ[ent] symbols to make larger numbers.

ANCIENT EGYPT

In around 3000 BCE, the Egyptians created a measuring system using cubits - the length of a man's forearm. The numbers one to nine were represented by **strokes** and larger numbers were shown using different **symbols**.

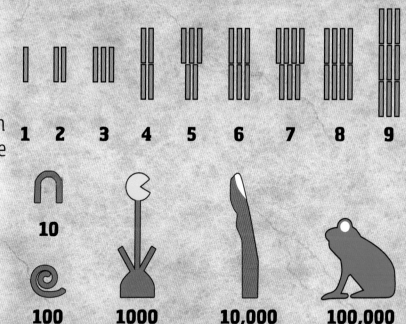

| 1 | 2 | 3 | 4 | 5 | 6 | 7 | 8 | 9 |

10

100

1000

10,000

100,000

ROMAN NUMERALS

Roman numerals used a combination of seven letters from the Latin alphabet - **I, V, X, L, C, D, M.** It was a fairly simple counting system and only really used for adding and subtracting. Roman numerals are still occasionally used today, particularly on clocks and to show dates.

MCMXXVII

These are the Roman numerals for the year 1927.

ARABIC NUMERALS

The next big advance in mathematics came in **India** in around 500 BCE. Symbols were created for every value from one to nine. Around 1200 CE, Arabic numerals spread into Europe and they are the numbers we use today.

THE BIRTH OF **MATHS**

Once people had established a system of **writing** numbers they began to think about how numbers could be used to explain things. Using numbers is called **mathematics**.

ANCIENT MATHS

The **ancient Greeks** developed sophisticated mathematical thinking. The Greek mathematician **Pythagoras** founded a school of maths and believed that maths ruled the Universe.

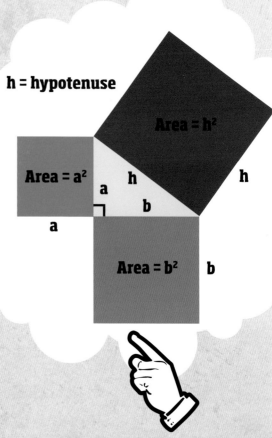

h = hypotenuse

Area = h^2

Area = a^2

h

a

b

a

Area = b^2

b

h

Pythagoras is famous for his theorem for right-angled triangles: the square of the hypotenuse is equal to the sum of the squares of the other two sides!
$$a^2 + b^2 = h^2$$

Archimedes is considered the father of mathematics.
A crater on the Moon and an asteroid are named in his honour!

Eureka!

ARCHIMEDES

Archimedes was another ancient Greek who played games with numbers and number patterns. He created many theories we still use today.

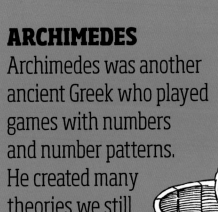

He is famous for working out a way of finding the **volume of an object.** He had his idea when he was in his bath and saw how the water was displaced by his body.

ALGEBRA

The **Arab world** was responsible for the invention of **algebra**. The word comes from the name of a book called *Al-Jabr,* written by the scholar Al Khwarizmi. His writings also included an explanation of the use of zero.

Al Khwarizmi

Algebra uses letters and symbols to represent unknown numbers.

UNUSUAL NUMBERS

Sometimes, words or phrases are used to describe **particular numbers**. Some are still used today, but most of them are not used in mathematics any more.

Astrologers use the dozen signs of the zodiac to describe the cycles of the Moon.

DOZEN

A *dozen* means **twelve**. The English word 'dozen' comes from the old French word 'douzaine'. This number was used in ancient times, and historians have suggested that it was used as a grouping because there are approximately **twelve cycles of the Moon in each cycle of the Sun** - or, as we now call it, a year.

THAT'S GROSS!

A *gross* is a dozen dozen, or **12 x 12 = 144**. It was often used for buying things in bulk, or for packing and shipping. There was also a **small gross**, which was **120**, and a **great gross**, which was **1728** - twelve lots of 144.

BAKER'S DOZEN

A baker's dozen actually means **thirteen**. It was invented by bakers, who would give their customers one extra loaf, cake or bun in their orders.

In the 13th century, bakers who short-changed customers were given very harsh penalties - which could even include having a hand chopped off. The extra item was a way of keeping their hands!

THE ARRIVAL OF THE

For thousands of years, people have built **machines** to help them with **maths**. These have ranged from simple **counting beads** to the latest **computers**.

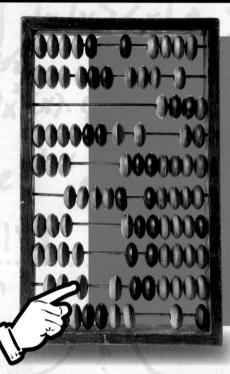

Beads are moved across the top bar to count objects. When all the top beads have moved, a bead is moved across on the next bar down.

The first known tool to aid calculation was the abacus, developed over 4000 years ago in China.

Slide rules were used before calculators were invented. Parts of the rule slid up and down against each other, lining up numbers to produce the result.

CALCULATOR

0.7734

ELECTRONIC MATHS

The first calculators were developed in the 1960s and were powered by mains electricity, but this was soon replaced by batteries. Some calculators even use **solar power**. Since the end have been widely used in schools.

The calculator has made maths easier for everyone, from school students to scientists!

MOBILE MATHS

Today, basic small calculators are cheap and easily available. However, many people carry out calculations on other machines and devices, such as their computer or mobile phone.

COMPUTING AND

The first **mechanical computer** was invented by Charles Babbage. Before that, a 'computer' was a person who added and subtracted numbers, writing the results on long tables.

DIFFERENCE ENGINE

In 1819, Babbage visited Paris and saw human 'computers' putting together scientific tables. He wondered if there was a way to produce the tables faster and more accurately. He invented the mechanised Difference Engine, which could solve complicated calculations by using repeated addition.

Long tables printed in books were used to work out complicated calculations, such as taxes.

BIG NUMBERS

Babbage later developed the Analytical Engine, which could multiply and divide and perform other general computing functions. It also had many of the features found in the modern digital computer – it could be programmed (using cards with holes punched in them) and it had a memory where numbers and solutions could be stored.

SUPERCOMPUTERS

Today, powerful computers can do **trillions of sums in a second**, allowing people to work out problems that would take years to solve. They are used to predict the weather or to work out how the stars and planets move.

A PIECE OF **PI** π

Pi is the ratio of a circle's circumference to its diameter, and is roughly **3.14**. That means, if you measure the **circumference** of a circle (all the way round the circle) and divide by the **diameter** (the distance across the circle) you get the number Pi.

Circumference

Diameter

Radius

π

Since the mid-1700s, the number Pi has been represented by this symbol.

There is no pattern in the digits of Pi - they go on and on without repeating any sequences.

3.141592653589793238449445923078164062862
306647093844609550
2110555964462294895
4337867831652712019091

If you drew a circle with a **diameter of one,** the **circumference would be equivalent to Pi.** So if you drew a circle in sand, and the diameter of the circle measured 1 metre, the circumference would be 3.14 metres.

Circumference = 3.14 m

Diameter = 1 m

The **radius** is half the distance across a circle. So if you drew a circle with a radius of 1 metre, the distance around half the edge of the circle would be 3.14 metres.

3.14 m

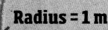
Radius = 1 m

PALINDROMIC NUMBERS

A palindrome is a word, phrase or number that reads the same whether it is read **backwards** or **forwards**:

Turn this number backwards and it still reads '1995991'.

BACKWARDS TIME
Sometimes you see palindromic numbers on a 24-hour clock.

BACKWARDS DATES
Sometimes we can see palindromic number phrases in dates. For example, 20:02 on the 20th February 2002 would be:
2002 2002 2002

ONE AND TWO DIGITS

All one-digit numbers in the decimal system are palindromic. Then there are nine two-digit numbers that are palindromic.

THREE DIGITS

There are **90 palindromic numbers** with three digits: **101, 111, 121, …, 989, 999.**
There are **nine** possible choices for the first digit (1 2 3 4 5 6 7 8 9) – and that determines the third digit, because it has to be the same. There are **10** possible choices for the second digit, as zero is included. Multiply these two numbers and you get:

$$9 \times 10 = 90$$

HUGE PALINDROMES

A palindromic number has no practical use in mathematics – but that doesn't stop people having fun with them! There are competitions to see who can create the longest – Harvey Duner created a palindromic number with 39,027 digits!

WORD PALINDROMES

Words can be palindromes, too:

MADAM

Palindromes can also be phrases. Edward Benbow created text containing 22,500 words to make an enormous palindromic composition.

FIBONACCI NUMBERS

In 1202, the Italian mathematician **Leonardo Bigollo**, also known as **Fibonacci**, introduced a number sequence to Europe – the **next number** is found by adding the value of the two that come before it.

0, **1,** 0+1 = **1,** 1+1 = **2,** 1+2 = **3,** 2+3 = **5,** 3+5 = **8**

NUMBERS IN NATURE

Fibonacci sequences can be found in lots of interesting places. For example, some plants grow stems, with the number of branches creating a Fibonacci sequence at different levels.

13

8

5

3

2

1

NUMBER SPIRAL

Fibonacci numbers do interesting things when they are arranged visually. Drawing squares whose sides follow the sequence creates an arrangement like this. Drawing a line between the corners then creates a spiral.

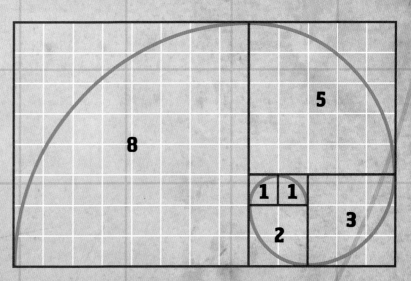

13, 21, 34, 55, 89, 144, 233...

FIBONACCI PLANTS

Fibonacci spirals are also found in **nature**, such as the arrangement of **pine cones** and the flowers of **artichokes**. The leaves of these grow around central stems in spirals that follow the **Fibonacci sequence**.

THE GOLDEN RATIO

The 'golden ratio' is a special number that is used in art and architecture as well as mathematics. The concept of the golden ratio has been known for at least 2400 years.

The golden ratio can be calculated by dividing any line into two uneven parts. When the longer part is divided by the shorter part, it should produce the same result as the entire line divided by the longer part. That answer is approximately **1.618**.

$$\frac{a}{b} = \frac{c}{a} = 1.618$$

So if you had a stick that was 3.236 metres long, you could divide it as follows:

a = 2 m, b = 1.236 m

2 ÷ 1.236 = 1.618

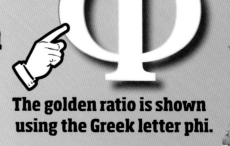

The golden ratio is shown using the Greek letter phi.

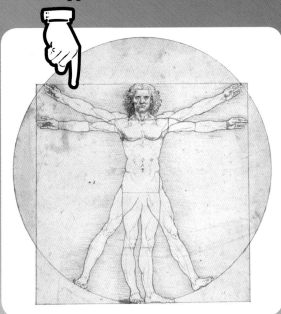

Leonardo da Vinci drew this figure and suggested that proportions in the human body show the golden ratio. For example, the ratio between the hand and forearm and the upper arm is about 1.618.

GOLDEN SPIRAL

Using the golden ratio will create a spiral similar to the Fibonacci sequence. In nature, **nautilus shells** (above) follow this spiral, as does the **cochlea** in your ear. It can also be seen in some spider webs.

BEAUTIFUL BUILDINGS

Artists and architects have long used the golden ratio in their paintings and buildings – including the Parthenon in Athens (left) – because it is thought to produce the most beautiful results.

$$a \div b = 1.618$$

a

GOD'S NUMBER

A team of researchers has now shown that no matter how scrambled a Rubik's Cube is, it can be solved in **20 moves** or less. This has been called '**God's Number**'.

COMPUTER CRUNCHING

Researchers worked out God's Number with a little help from a bank of computers. The solution took **35 CPU-years** to solve! CPU means Central Processing Unit - the part of a computer that 'thinks' and works things out. The amount of work a CPU can do depends on how many streams it can handle. A CPU that can handle three streams will do three CPU-years of work in a normal year.

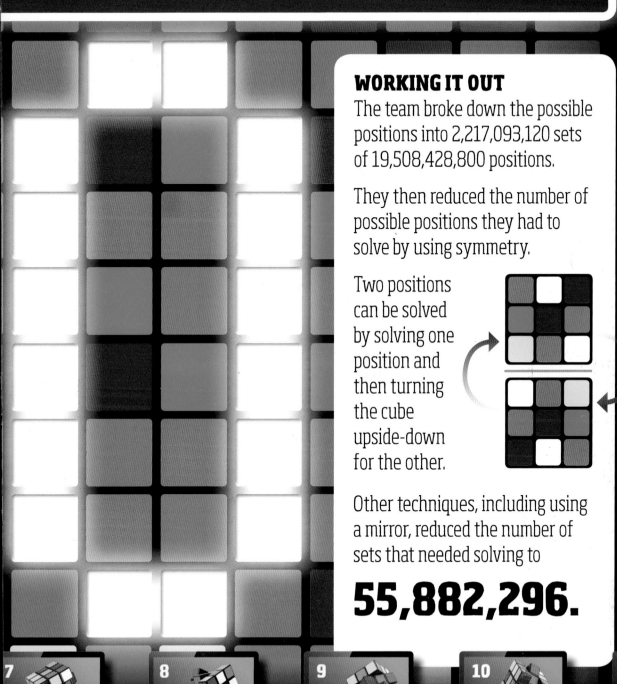

WORKING IT OUT

The team broke down the possible positions into 2,217,093,120 sets of 19,508,428,800 positions.

They then reduced the number of possible positions they had to solve by using symmetry.

Two positions can be solved by solving one position and then turning the cube upside-down for the other.

Other techniques, including using a mirror, reduced the number of sets that needed solving to

55,882,296.

THE **RECORD-BREAKING**

Here are some **record-breaking** numbers about the amazing Rubik's Cube.

Three-year-old Ruxin Liu is the **youngest person** to solve the Rubik's Cube in an amazing **1 minute** and **39.33 seconds**

The smallest cube is a tiny **10 millimetres** wide, and was created by Russian puzzle builder Evgeniy Grigoriev.

ACTUAL SIZE!

The current **world record** for solving the Rubik's Cube is **00m 05.55s** ...that's fast!

RUBIK'S CUBE

The **world's most expensive Rubik's Cube** is encrusted with jewels! It is a fully functioning cube, but at around **£1.5 million,** it is an expensive toy! It features:

 34 carats of emeralds

 22.5 carats of amethysts

 34 carats of rubies

 all set in 18-carat gold

3 metres

The **biggest** cube ever made is in Tennessee in the USA. It weighs 500 kilograms, and is **3 metres tall** – the same height as an elephant!

OTHER **RUBIK'S PUZZLES**

Now you have solved your **Rubik's Cube**, there are plenty of other 3D puzzles to play with, stretch your maths abilities and give you hours of **entertainment**.

As the player moves the spheres of the Rubik's 360, they twist and turn, as they are weighted. That makes it hard to solve!

THE RUBIK'S 360

Ernö Rubik also invented a puzzle called the **Rubik's 360**, which went on sale in 2009. It is made up of three clear balls, which contain six small coloured balls. To solve the puzzle you have to move the coloured balls from the inner ball to the outer ball, and trap them in a dome shape.

THE TWIST

Rubik has also invented the **Twist-Limited** - a twistable set of joined triangles that can be made into lots of different shapes. It is designed to be an educational tool that helps the player think about spaces and shapes.

There are no wrong answers to the Twist, but it comes with a booklet showing different shapes.

DIGITAL PUZZLES

Rubik's Race is a new puzzle that's available both as a board game and an app. Competitors can go head-to-head or against the clock to re-create a random pattern.

The Rubik's Race app allows players to slide coloured tiles around the screen.

BEST TIME
CURRENT TIME
00:01.57

RUBIK'S SLIDING PUZZLES

Not content with puzzling people in **three dimensions**, Ernö Rubik has also developed a couple of fiendish 2D puzzles.

RUBIK'S FIFTEEN

The Rubik's Cube is not the only puzzle invented by Ernö Rubik. **The Rubik's Fifteen** has 17 sliding tiles on a **5 x 5 square.** The tiles are numbered one to fifteen in roman numerals, plus an asterisk and a black square. They are moved around the square using levers.

DOUBLE TROUBLE

The Rubik's Fifteen contains **two different puzzles,** one on either side of the square. The back of the square is a window with a small **3 x 3 square.** It can be solved as a magic square.

You cannot complete both Rubik's Fifteen puzzles at the same time.

RUBIK'S MAGIC

Launched in the mid-1980s, the Rubik's Magic consists of **eight square tiles**. The aim is to fold the tiles until the picture on the top shows the three rings linked together.

The grooves in each of the tiles hold wires so that the tiles can be folded and unfolded.

There are an amazing

11,381,997,699,072,000

possible positions for the tiles in Rubik's Magic – although this isn't as many as the Rubik's Cube's 43 quintillion possible combinations.

GLOSSARY

Big Bang
The Universe was created when there was a huge explosion billions of years ago. Scientists and astronomers call the explosion the Big Bang.

Census
A census is a way of collecting information about the population of a country. Information is collected about the age, occupation and gender of the people who are surveyed.

Currency
Currency is the money - coins and notes - that is made by a country to represent value. They are tokens exchanged for things in shops, and the money that people earn.

Decimal
Decimal means based on the number ten. The numbers we use in everyday life are decimal numbers. 'Decimal number' sometimes means a number that uses a decimal point followed by digits that represent a value less than one, such as 3.25.

Dozen
Dozen means twelve. This is an old-fashioned word for the number, which is not often used today.

Fibonacci sequence
A series or pattern of numbers identified by the Italian mathematician known as Fibonacci. It is created by adding the sum of the two numbers previous to find the next number.

Finite
When something has an end, and can be measured, counted or given a value.

Fraction
Part of a whole. The bottom number is called the denominator, and shows how many parts the whole number is divided into. The top number is called the numerator, and says how many parts of a whole are in the fraction.

Googol

A googol is the number represented by one followed by 100 zeros.

Googolplex

A googolplex is the number represented by one followed by a googol zeros.

Gross

A gross is an old-fashioned word meaning 144. It is not often used today.

Infinity

When something goes on forever, without ending.

Inflation

A general rise in the cost of things.

Light year

A light year is a unit of distance used in astronomy. It is equal to the distance travelled by light in one year.

Negative numbers

Numbers with a value that is less than zero. They are shown with a minus sign in front of them.

Palindromic numbers

Palindromic numbers are the same read backwards or forwards.

Pi

In mathematics, Pi (3.14) is the number that represents the relation between the circumference of a circle and its diameter.

Place value

The value of a digit within a number is determined by its place within that number, such as units, tens or hundreds.

Population

The population of a country means all the people who live there.

Positive numbers

Numbers with a value that is greater than zero. They are sometimes shown with a plus sign.

Statistics

The collection, study and explanation of data (information).

Vertices

The vertices of a shape are the corners, where three or more edges meet.

INDEX